Latter-day Grooks 5

Bill Wylson

Other Books by Bill Wylson

Hieroglyphs, Golden Plates & Typos

Give Place in Your Heart

Three Minutes Eighteen Seconds

Elder Hammond and The Inspector

The Manger on The Mantle

Latter-day Grooks Vol. I, II, III & IV

Available at:

www.billwylsonbooks.com

First Edition published May 2025

White Horse Books
Salt Lake City, Utah

"*If your life is a leaf
That the seasons tear off and condemn,
[He] will bind you with love
That is graceful and green as a stem.*"
L. Cohen

www.greenstemmedia.com

Table of Contents

What is a Grook?

A grook is a short poem with an aphoristic essence. Grooks were initially created by the Danish poet Piet Hein (1905–1996), who wrote over 10,000 in Danish and English. A grook, known as 'gruk' in the Danish language, is a unique literary art form. It is a condensed poetic expression that captures profound meaning in just a few lines. Grooks put pertinent new perspectives on everyday observations, presenting the reader with small instructions on the art of living.

The beauty of this style lies not only in its brevity but also in how it presents wisdom and philosophical insights. Usually expressed in rhyme, these poetry pieces embody cultural or broader life truths. Through simple yet resonant language, grooks encapsulate significant sentiments that make readers deeply contemplate life's various themes and experiences.

Piet Hein, a descendant of Piet Pieterszoon Hein, the 17th-century Dutch naval hero, was born in Copenhagen, Denmark. He studied at the Institute for Theoretical Physics of the University of Copenhagen (later to become the Niels Bohr Institute) and the Technical University of Denmark. In 1972, Yale awarded him an honorary doctorate.

One of the author's favorite Piet Hein grooks is entitled:

Problems

Problems worthy
of attack
prove their worth
by hitting back.

What is a Latter-day Grook?

As Latter-day Saints, we have a distinctive collection of wisdom and insight exclusive to our faith. It is the revealed truth bestowed upon Latter-day prophets and apostles. This canon is unique and significant within our religious tradition, yet it remains primarily unacquainted to the outside world.

This literature contains profound wisdom concerning life's most significant existential questions. It addresses themes like morality, righteousness, faith, and divinity. The knowledge revealed in our literature is deeply rooted in our theology.

It is often easier to recall essential writings when they appear in poetic form because poetry resonates with us. We enjoy reading or hearing something that reflects our thinking and feelings. I sincerely pray that the message of these Latter-day Grooks will be bound to our hearts and minds and offer us hope, strength, and encouragement in resisting evil, overcoming the world, and drawing nearer to God.

"Keep thy father's commandment, and forsake not the law of thy mother:

"Bind them continually upon thine heart, and tie them about thy neck.

"When thou goest, it shall lead thee; when thou sleepest, it shall keep thee; and when thou awakest, it shall talk with thee."

Proverbs 6:20-22.

Politics

Patriotic Grook

United we stand,
divided we fall,
and the powers that be
are dividing us all.

Hold On!

When the reasoning
      of men overrides
the revelations given by God,

then the proud will find
      he backslides
and lets go of the iron rod.

Rest When It Rains

To prevent any harm
to their delicate wings,
butterflies rest
whenever there's rain.

So, when storms are what
your troubled life brings,
rest for a while.
You'll soon fly again.

I
II
III
IV
V
VI
VII
VIII
IX
X

A Simple Truth

Here is a truth
to keep in mind—
a commandment broken
is a blessing declined.

Killer

Each of us should fear it,
more than a gun
      or a bomb or a knife,

for the unforgiving spirit
is the number one
      killer of a spiritual life.

You Are Kind

Something you should take note of
And always keep in mind:

Kindness should have no motive.
Be kind because you *are* kind.

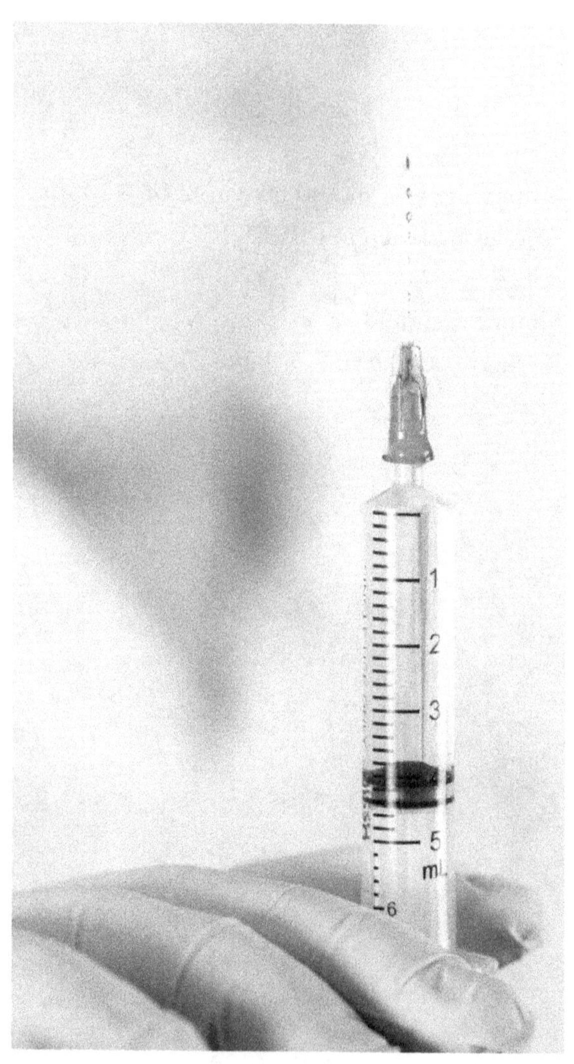

No Cure

29

There is no cure
for the ills of the world,
except for the light
of the gospel of Christ.

Service Grook

An axiom true as life itself,
(as I'm sure you will observe)
we don't mature stuck on a shelf,
we only grow as we serve.

Modern-day Prophets

In an often-futile attempt to aid them
they call on all people to repent,
to worship the God who made them,
and believe in those whom He has sent.

Worldly Pleasure

Worldly pleasure
      is but an instant.
The joy of the gospel
      is eternal and constant.

Revelation from God

Pure knowledge
is far greater than
the limited reasoning
of mortal man.

Growth by Degrees

For the work of the Lord to advance
by any measure or degree,
it must not be done happenstance,
but deliberately—by you and me.

Unlimited Truth

Limited knowledge
is a dangerous thing
considering the damage
partial truths can bring.

Teach Them Early

Parents, please don't wait till
your child is ready to shave.
"Faith-building begins in the cradle
and ends not at the grave." [1]

---

[1] Young, S. Dilworth.

Constitutional Grook

If we don't save our Constitution
from menacing dangers that threaten it,
we will one day wake up to find
we have a whole new government.

Full Salvation

Full salvation preserved
throughout time and all eternity
is obtained only in and through
the exalted eternal family.

FEAR
DIVORCE
STOCK MARKET CRASH
$ $ $ CORPORATE GREED $ $ $ $
SICKNESS AND DISEASE
FRAUD
RIPTION
UGS
UNEMPLOYMENT
DE PRESS ION
JOBLESS
VIOLENCE
DECEPTION
NTAMINATED WATER
ANIMAL ABUSE
CHAOS
STARVATION
SECRET POLICE
MONEY IS A LIE
COLLEGE IS A SCAM
GLOBAL WARFARE
CRIME
APE
BANKRUPTCY
POLITICAL SELL-OUT
FAT

A World in Trouble

This is a world in difficulty and trouble,
but we shouldn't bemoan the fact.
We should, as far as our powers allow us,
be anxiously engaged in rectifying that.

Secret Combinations

The Book of Mormon's vocabulary
garnishes no conspiracy theory,
though you'll find its pages amply stacked
with a fair amount of conspiracy fact.

From the Sacred Grove

No longer is He
a missing God or absentee.
He reveals Himself today to be
a living, divine reality.

Judge Not

More and more, it seems apparent
this gift is such a rarity—
but only in *not* passing judgment
do we display true charity.

The Lord Helps Those...

Pray for the righteous
desires of your heart,
then boost that request
by doing your part.

Confirming Witness

*"What greater witness can you have
than from God?"* [2]

That burning sensation
you feel when kneeling
is a confirming witness—
not merely a feeling.

[2] D&C 6:23.

Exaltation

Through the grace of God,
the gift is given.

Through obedience, we claim
our inheritance in Heaven.

Freedom Grook

Without the spirit of freedom
in the souls of mortal man,
there could be no willing response
to the Savior's perfect plan.

The Voice

"I testify that if we shall look to the First Presidency,
we shall gain peace in this life and ... eternal glory in
the world to come." [3]

For the saints and the world to stay
on the path the Lord wants us to be,
we must listen to and always obey
the voice of the First Presidency.

---

[3] Smith, Joseph Fielding.

Suicides Anonymous

"I am convinced that many in the Church are committing spiritual suicide, and they are calling for help, just like those who are going to commit suicide physically." [4]

Many among us today indicate
the cry of spiritual suicide.
If we hear their cry before it's too late,
we can become their saving guide.

---

[4] Lee, Harold B.

They Do as They Please

The unenlightened and spiritually misguided
demand what *they* call 'free agency.'

It seems that they have already decided
right is wrong, and virtue—indecency.

I CAN DO
EVERYTHING
THROUGH
HIM WHO
GIVES ME
STRENGTH
Philippians 4:13

The Best We Can

It is not enough
to do our best,
that's a lesson
we must be taught;

for unless we do
all we can, then
we often do less
than we ought.

The Atonement

The center of all good things,
as far at least as I have learned,
is the Lord's atoning sacrifice,
as far as the saints are concerned.

Anyone Could Start a Church, But...

You can't take a living branch
from the trunk of a dead, rotting tree,

nor can you act in God's Holy Name
without having His power and authority.

Havano Shalo Malechem

Don't just sing, "Let there be peace on earth and let it begin with me," but mean it. [5]

There would be peace in every family
if each person had peace in their soul.
And if there were peace in every family,
there'd be peace in the nation as a whole.
If there were peace in every nation, then
there'd be peace in the world.
Let *that* be our goal.

---

[5] Smith, Eldred G.

The Price of Sin

The diseases of sin and ignorance
make us scream and holler and fuss.

We rarely get ulcers from what we eat;
we get ulcers from what's eating at us.

Precious Possessions

Civilizations perish, monuments fall,
nothing humans build will ever last.

But perusing a great book is like a stroll
with the noblest minds of the past.

Dwell Forever

Let Thy Spirit dwell in our hearts
and when the trials of life are over,

may we return to Thy holy presence
and dwell in Thy house forever.

By Grace, We Are Saved

You may think that it is irony
but salvation cannot be bought

even with the hard-earned currency
of doing that which we ought.

In The Shadow

If we look for joy in possessions,
or seek for peace in our pride,
we will find we are always at a loss—

True peace lies in the intercession
of the love and mercy applied
in the shadow of a stark wooden cross.

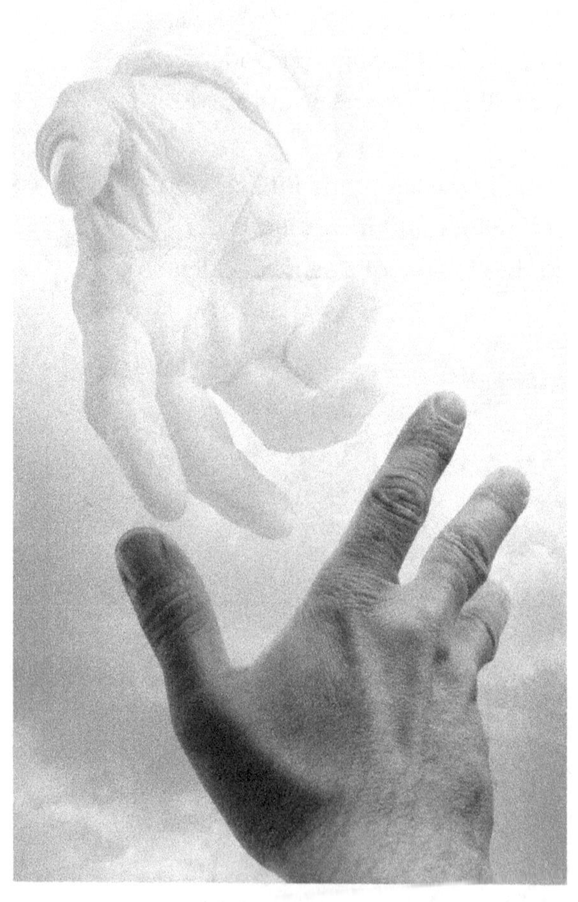

God Exists

God exists in the world
despite the deniers,
wherever, whenever we need Him—

for the humble seekers
with pressing desires,
for the ones who genuinely heed Him.

Innocent Young Spirits

Banks hold in trust
precious worldly assets,
things of value belonging to others.

God holds in trust
His most precious possessions
in the hands of earthly fathers and mothers.

Reports of Imperfection

That we have not found perfection
in men or church or fellowship—
this is no reason for rejection
of our need to seek, to serve, to worship.

Cleansing Forgiveness

All of us have made mistakes,
(Some, enough to fill an ocean!)

But all of us, too, can be forgiven
Through repentance and earnest devotion.

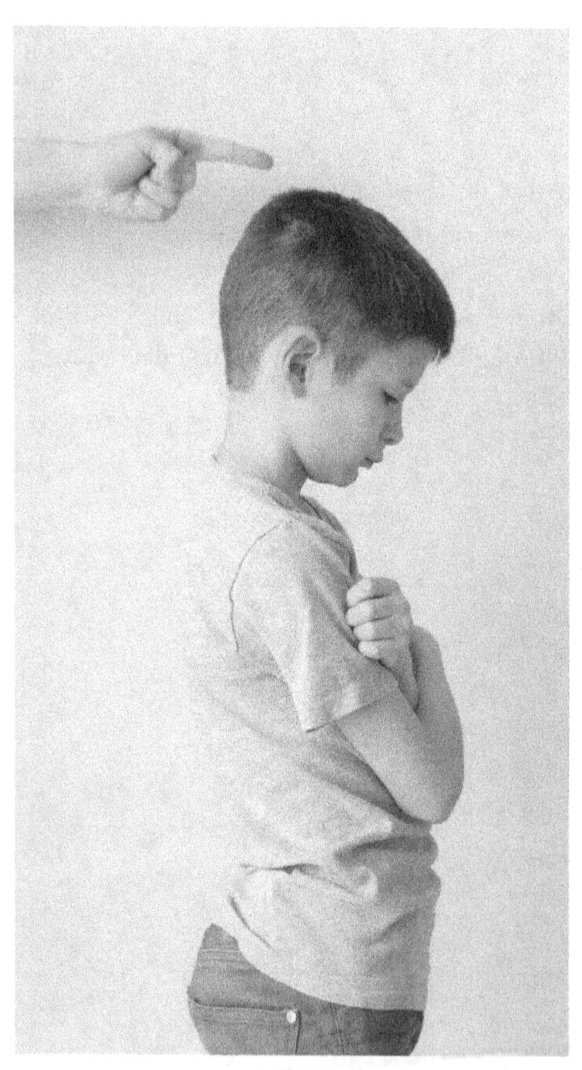

The Loss of the Crown

97

Often, very often, though we may
attempt somehow to ignore them,

we are punished as much *by* our sins
as we are punished for them.

To Know God

Knowing God does not solve life's problems
or hardly even hamper them,
but it gives us the purpose and the strength
we surely need to master them.

Repent!

Repentance is a refining force,
made possible through Jesus Christ.
It purifies mortal minds and bodies,
revealing godlike natures and qualities
so that with God, we can enjoy eternal life.

HAPPY
TRUTH
TRUTH
BELIEVE

Still Believin'

The frailties or failings of others
can never be an appropriate reason
for losing the blessings we might have
by doing our duty and still believin'.

Act

A simple suggestion:
Never delay
a sincere impression
to stop and pray.

Gallop Poll

We want to know what
Republicans and Democrats think.
We're interested in what
unions, economists, and diplomats think.
But amid all the worldly,
political, and social high jinx,
we ought to strive, above all else,
to know what God our Father thinks.

Grateful Partakers

May God help us to be more grateful
for the saving truths of the gospel of Christ,
and may we more worthily eat the bread
and freely drink the waters of life.

I Need Thee

God may not need me
to perform the work
      that He is currently addressing,

but I do need God
and the strength I receive
      from His kind and gracious blessing.

By His Grace

Is it only the perfect
who make it to Heaven?

No—it is all us sinners
who have been frankly forgiven.

The Importance of Testimony

The strength of the Church
depends upon me and you
coming to know for ourselves
that this restored gospel is true.

Allegiance Grook

Some words, it seems,
become invisible,
Like 'under God'
And 'indivisible.'

GOD
loves
YOU

Lost in Translation

When God or
His servants cry
"Repent! Repent!"

Remember,
"I love you! I love you!"
is what they meant.

Called to Serve

When anxiety surfaces
remember this saying:
Spectacular purposes
require spectacular praying.

Don't Give Up

When you attract the devil's attention,
don't give up, and don't stand still.
It could be a clear indication
that what you're doing is God's will.

Pray Always

If daily prayer seems a burden
or too troublesome a task,
remember, God seldom gives answers
to questions we didn't ask.

today's
plan

Eternal Possessions

Eternal progress seems to suggest
we should try to live diurnally
with all the resolves and purposes
we want to possess eternally.

Thoughts and Prayers

Good thoughts, warm feelings, and passionate
prayers
which well-intended, idle people pursue,
can never come close or ever equal
the inclination to just "go and do."

The Voice We Heed

If our lives are not aligned with Christ,
we could make poor, improper choices—
not because we're bad people at heart
but because we heed improper voices.

Follow Me
Jesus

The Task

We feast upon the words of Christ,
make covenants and renew them.
The task now is to take His words
and "see that ye [actually] do them."

The Glad Reaper

*"All of us have, in one sense or another, reaped where
we have not sown and harvested where we did not
plant."* [6]

Every life that ever appeared
on this earthly shelf
has been enriched and endeared
by someone other than self.

---

[6] Wylson, Bill. *Give Place in Your Heart*

I hope you have enjoyed this little volume.

Please post an honest 5-star review on a book site where you have posting privileges. You could mention which grook was your favorite.

If you found this book enjoyable, inspirational, educational, or enlightening, please tell your friends about it.

About the Author

Bill Wylson is the author of over 50 published works on family values, religious issues, and religious education. His work has appeared in *The Ensign, This People, The New Era, Liberty Magazine, Success,* and others.

Bill graduated from the *Columbia School of Broadcasting* in Hollywood, CA, as a commercial copywriter. He wrote trade journal ads for a major advertising agency in Los Angeles and public service announcements for a Los Angeles television station.

He has served as a volunteer Board Member of *Advocates of Single Parent Youth, Special Fun Games for the Disabled*, and on the Boards of Arts and Theater Councils. He has also served on Advisory Committees for the *Volunteer Center of Los Angeles* and on the *United Way Government Affairs Committee.*

Bill Wylson lives in Salt Lake City, Utah.

Other Books by Bill Wylson

Give Place in Your Heart:
31 Promises from the Book of Mormon

All of us are familiar with Moroni's promise that Christ will manifest the truth of the Book of Mormon to us by the power of the Holy Ghost. This is just one of many promises the Lord has made regarding the Book of Mormon.

The concepts presented in this book encourage personal growth and self-reflection. By recognizing the conditions attached to each promise from the Lord, readers can make positive changes that enhance their spiritual character.

In *Give Place in Your Heart*, Bill Wylson outlines 31 promises, with their attendant blessings and conditions, that the Lord would love to bestow upon you.

Latter-day Grooks
Volumes One, Two, Three, and Four

Grooks were originally created by the Danish poet Piet Hein, (1905–1996) who wrote over 10,000 of them in both the Danish and English languages. A grook ('gruk' in Danish) is a form of short aphoristic poem or rhyming aphorism.

Literary experts suggest that the term 'gruk' is a compilation of the Danish words 'GRin and sUK', meaning to laugh and sigh. Grooks are multi-faceted and are meant to be spirit-building. They are often characterized by irony, paradox, brevity, precise use of language, rhythm, and rhyme.

In these volumes, Bill Wylson has attempted to cite the words and teachings from the Church of Jesus Christ of Latter-day Saints and to express these ideas in the form of latter-day grooks.

Words are extremely powerful. Lord Byron poetically portrays this truth:

"But words are things, and a small drop of ink,
Falling like dew, upon a thought, produces
That which makes thousands, perhaps millions,
think."

Three Minutes Eighteen Seconds examines three "small drops of ink" that are simultaneously extremely powerful words spoken by President Thomas S. Monson at the April 2017 General Conference, his final message to the people of this world.

On the inside cover of his first leather-bound Book of Mormon, my father had written the following quotation from the prophet Joseph Smith:

"I told the brethren that the Book of Mormon was the most correct of any book on earth, and the keystone of our religion, and a man would get nearer to God by abiding by its precepts, than by any other book."

Directly below this quote, my father had compiled a list of scriptures labeled: "Mistakes in the Book of Mormon."

Committing his writings to the future reader, Moroni candidly and apologetically acknowledged: *"And if there be faults they be the faults of a man. But behold, we know no fault."* How did my father have the audacity to make a list of mistakes in the Book of Mormon? To better understand these 'corrections' in the Book of Mormon and how they testify to its truthfulness and authenticity, we need to understand the process involved in making plates of ore and the method for inscribing on them.

Elder Hammond and the Inspector

"You know, there's a word to describe someone who won't even bother to meet you at the bus station. It starts with an 'O' or, I don't know, maybe a 'C' or something. I think it's C-a—. No, I've lost it."

Elder Hammond was a freckled-face, shy sort of bumpkin from some rural farm town in Kansas. He was awkward and withdrawn. Even in his white shirt and tie, he reminded you of the type of kid you'd see in denim coveralls, wearin' a straw hat and chompin' on a thin blade of grass whilst irrigatin' the lower forty.

I knew nothing about Elder Hammond's personal life. He was just a simple, quiet, humble boy, determined and dedicated. He had no delusions of grandeur, just a desire to serve. Perhaps more than any missionary, Elder Hammond had a purity of spirit and an altruistic motivation in ministering. I pitied him. I think he actually believed he could make a difference.

The Manger on the Mantle
A Christmas Tale based on Two True Stories

The Manger on the Mantle recounts the tragic life of Mark Spencer, a man raised in a small town who somehow becomes very lost in the massive city of Los Angeles. He didn't become geographically lost; he became spiritually lost.

As his family falls apart and his world collapses, Mark realizes just how tainted his life has become. He has strayed so far from the innocence of his youth, and now he fears he may never find his way back.

That's when Mark meets Marvin, a sockless, root-beer- float-toting ex-hippie. Together, they journey the road to Bethlehem as they ponder the purpose of a birth in a lowly manger.

The Manger on the Mantle is a beautiful story of hope and redemption and the joyous possibility of being given a second chance.

Climate change is real and is not just a distant threat; it is a pressing issue that we need to address now. There should be no debate about this. However, views on climate issues are often polarized, ranging from the causes and solutions for climate change to trust and skepticism regarding climate scientists and their research.

According to NASA, "Climate change is one of the most complex issues facing us today. It involves many dimensions—science, economics, society, politics, and moral and ethical questions—and is a global problem, felt on local scales. This challenge will persist for decades and centuries to come."

The only real question we should focus on is: "What can we do about it?" The answer may surprise you.